MIND FREEDOM:
Re-program Yourself for Success and Happiness with Meditations, Affirmations, & Mindset Shifts

ROB CUBBON

Mind Freedom: Re-program Yourself for Success and Happiness with Meditations, Affirmations, Mindset Shifts
Rob Cubbon
Published by Rob Cubbon Ltd. *http://robcubbon.com*
© 2015 © 2016 Rob Cubbon
No portion of this publication may be reproduced or transmitted in any form or by any means, electronic or mechanical, including, but not limited to, audio recordings, facsimiles, photocopying, or information storage and retrieval systems without explicit written permission from the author or publisher.
ISBN-13: 978-1541337442
ISBN-10: 1541337441

Contents page

Introduction	5
Baiyoke sky hotel, Bangkok, Thailand	6
Crouch End, London, UK. Ten years ago.	8
Before we start	13
A Counter-Intuitive View on Time	16
Don't believe the hype	18
Ignore everything you have no control over	20
Moonbeach Bungalows, Phangan Cove, Koh Phangan	25
A life outside labels	27
How does this help us?	30
Do the following to free up time and energy	32
Meditation	38
Affirmations	45
Mind and Body	56
Ban Tai Bungalows, Mae Nam, Koh Samui, the Gulf of Thailand	57
If what you're doing isn't working change what you're doing or how you're doing it	60
The Marriott, Cebu City, the Philippines	62
Putting it all together	66

Introduction

This booklet will add more freedom and happiness to your life.

We are all born free. We are all freer than we think we are. But sometimes when you get up for work in the morning, freedom seems like a privilege reserved for the rich and famous.

It isn't.

The freest people in the world are usually neither rich nor famous.

I'm not rich but I'm free to enjoy extended vacations my business makes more than enough for me to live very comfortably. I'm not famous but I have cultivated a small following online, which is largely responsible for my income.

I'm here to help you on your journey to freedom.

The following advice is not only my story; I've been extremely fortunate during the last few years to have connected with a large number of people who have been successful in finding freedom and happiness.

I've also met lots of people who are *trying* to achieve this freedom but are floundering. We've all been there; chasing shiny objects or walking dead-end paths. The goal of this booklet is to steer you in the right direction.

Thank you for reading this booklet's introduction. I urge you to continue and to follow some of the advice here. If you do, I promise you'll live with greater freedom of thought and happiness in your life.

Baiyoke Sky Hotel, Bangkok, Thailand

9:00am: I awake. Relaxed and alert, my brain goes through the usual process of familiarization: What beautiful part of Southeast Asia am I in today?

Do I have anything to do today? Strangely enough, I do. I have a flight booked to Koh Samui – a tropical paradise island in the Gulf of Thailand.

After a shower I go through my morning Tai Chi and meditation practice. Twenty minutes later I'm headed out for breakfast with my trusty backpack slung across one shoulder.

As I make my way through a cool and serene hotel lobby out into the warm Bangkok streets, I piece together what happened last night.

I remember having a few beers in a rooftop bar with an old friend from London. He had to pretend his grandmother was dying to get a measly two-week vacation from his job. I explained to him my life is a vacation, as we admired the Bangkok skyline.

In a café, I pull out my MacBook from my backpack and order a coffee. Once the laptop is connected to the café's Wi-Fi, I flick through tabs on my browser. I refresh my revenue reports on several websites to see the sales I've made since I last checked.

It's good news. An online learning platform that sells some of my video courses is running a special promotion that's netted me $150 in the last 12 hours. I check a few more sites. My Kindle sales are up, that's another $25.

I open my email. A quick scan reveals a PayPal email that means I've had a few sales on my own membership site. Another $150.

That's $325 since I'd checked before going out last night – more than enough to cover yesterday's beers, taxis, the hotel stay and today's plane ticket.

I can't imagine a life better than this one.

Crouch End, London, UK. Ten Years Ago.

My morning routine wasn't always so relaxed. I'd get up with a hangover and desperately try to fix a coffee before rushing from my suburban apartment to join other commuters on a bus journey to the underground train station.

In London, the underground train is called the "tube." At Finsbury Park, my nearest tube station, you walk through subterranean "tubes" to get to the platforms. Like blood cells pushed and sucked through veins, you have little choice about where you're going. You just follow everyone else.

Similarly, I thought I had little choice about my life at that time. I just followed everyone else.

We all have our moments of sleep-walking, but I somnambulated through life more than most. It was 2003, and I was doing tedious jobs in London.

Increasingly, I would escape the mind-numbing boredom by getting drunk in front of the TV every night. That didn't seem strange or dysfunctional to me at the time. After all, everyone around me was doing the same thing: going to work all day and getting smashed in their "free" time. I followed everyone else and I didn't question it.

I had no ambition or aspirations.

If I tried to excel at something, it was to excel at enjoying myself. I put all my efforts into being a good drinking companion and party animal.

My life quickly morphed into a routine of going to work on a train through a tube, spending eight hours or more inside an office, eating bad food, returning home through the same tube, then eating more bad food, watching TV and drinking beer.

It wasn't long before other stimulants were added to alcohol to enhance my mood.

I'd first started smoking cigarettes at 18. This quickly developed into a pack-a-day habit. I would also regularly smoke marijuana with tobacco rolled up in cigarette papers.

On weekends, I would indulge in ecstasy and cocaine. These so-called "white" drugs enhanced my mood even more than the cigarettes, weed and alcohol. They took things to another level. Being under the influence of ecstasy and cocaine would cause me to smoke and drink even more. The drug "comedowns" were worse than the alcohol hangovers. I used to have to drink more beer and smoke more marijuana in order to lessen the effects of the comedown. It would take me until Thursday or Friday to feel a bit better, and then the weekend binge would start again.

The drinking, the drugs, the cigarettes and the unhealthy eating should have been bad enough, but the worst was the negative self-talk.

"I'm young at the prime of my life. I should be happy, successful and enjoying an exuberant social and sex life," I would proclaim. So I saw a doctor and told her I was depressed. She gave me pills and booked me in to see a Cognitive Behavioural Therapist.

I saw the therapist once a week for a few months. We dragged up every unfortunate episode from my childhood I could remember. This didn't exorcise any demons; it just reinforced more memories I could feel sorry for myself about.

And that's where I was in 2003.

However, I gave up cigarettes, stopped taking drugs, reduced my drinking, cut down my negative self-talk, started a business and became a happier person.

How? I'm going to try to explain the first few steps…

Before We Start

Before we get going, I have some free gifts for you. Why? Well, I think you might like them, for one thing. But I have another reason: you'll have to enter your email address, which means I'll be able to keep you informed of my journey and help you further in yours.

Of course, I will not share your email address with anyone nor will I spam you with emails you don't want. You are free to unsubscribe at any time.

My website is at *http://robcubbon.com* —check it out and let me know what you think. And you *can sign up for my free newsletter* here at: *http://robcubbon.com/free*.

If you subscribe, you'll get:
- Free copies of my e-book PDFs: *How to Market Yourself Online* and *Starting An Online Business*
- Two MP3s about online business
- A list of my favorite online tools
- Notification of future free Kindle books and offers

If you're interested, sign up here: *http://robcubbon.com/free*. If not, that's cool too!

And that's not all. I also have some video courses that you can watch for free on my site. They could help you on your journey.

I have a free mini-course about how to earn passive income (that's making money from digital product sales where someone clicks a buy button and money ends up in your account while you're sleeping). There are also courses about WordPress website creation and email marketing – handy skills for setting up an online business and becoming free.

You can get these free courses here: *http://robcubbon.com/freecourses*

My journey towards freedom involved many stages.

I started by freeing my thoughts which gave me the calmness and mental capacity to start my own business. Starting my own business gave me greater financial freedom which allowed me to pursue passive income and experience yet more freedoms – the freedom of time and the freedom of location.

I'm free to do what I want, where I want, when I want, without worrying about money. How did I get there? It all started with freedom of thought, which is what this booklet is concerned with.

The Beginning of Freedom of Thought: It Starts with an Idea

All human endeavor starts with an idea. The invention of the wheel, mechanical computation, putting a man on the moon – these were all ideas before they became reality.

This is why you should have an idea for who you want to be.

Mindset is more important than technical ability, more important than people skills, and more important than any other capability you may have or may gain in the future.

If there's one thing I want you to know, it's this: you can do it.

You can achieve your highest aspirations and your most audacious dreams. You can improve your surroundings, you can become a happier person and you can draw in positive people and beneficial situations to your life. You can do all this yourself right now. You don't need anything else, anyone else or luck.

You can do it.

Believe you can do what you want. That's all you need. If you don't believe now, don't worry, because you can change your beliefs – I did.

I changed my thoughts and it led to creating websites, setting up a business, leaving work, traveling around the world and being happy. Without this mindset shift, I never would have even gotten started.

What was at the beginning of the mindset shift that saved me?

The belief that I could improve my life by my own efforts

and my own efforts alone.

My old belief – that a good life was caused by external stimuli – was all wrong. Good luck, bad luck or the situations you find yourself in are incidental. They appear as though they're affecting events but they aren't. You are.

I realised I could improve my mood by elevating my thoughts. I started to identify the first thoughts that would lead to a downward spiral of negative self-talk, and stopped myself as quickly as I could.

The negative self-talk was a familiar chorus: *"I was a failure at school, a failure with girls and now a failure at work."* Or maybe when something didn't go my way I would say to myself, *"Oh, that thing went wrong at work; I'm always making mistakes and I'm rubbish at what I do."*

But instead of slipping into that spiral, I now notice negative self-talk and try to stop it. I think about something different, concentrate on whatever I am doing at the moment and/or "reframe" the negativity into something neutral or positive.

An example of reframing would be: *"Maybe I was a failure at school, maybe I was a failure with girls, or maybe I wasn't. But I'm feeling OK at this present moment."*

This changed my life: identifying and noticing the negative self-talk and killing the ideas before they spiralled into more damaging thought processes and limiting beliefs.

Whenever you notice yourself thinking negatively, stop and **concentrate on the present moment.**

What do I mean by concentrating on the present moment? It's very easy. You can do it now, this very moment. Are you sitting down? Then notice the feeling of the chair on your ass. Notice the feeling of your clothes on your body. Or you can concentrate on the feeling of your breath on the inside of your nostrils passing in and out while you breathe.

The present moment is the most important time there is.

A Counter-Intuitive View on Time

Now that we're talking about the present moment, I'm going to introduce a concept that will seem alien to a lot of people. And it's this: The present moment is, in fact, the only time there is.

I know this is a difficult concept when you are first exposed to it. You'll say to me, "False! I'm 100% sure I woke up this morning and took the dog out." The past only exists in our thoughts (that includes your memory of this morning).

If you close your eyes and concentrate on the feeling of your body (ass or chair, clothes on body, air through nostrils) then, right at this moment, the past and future are irrelevant.

No two versions of history are ever the same. There is evidence of things having happened (old buildings, earthquake damage, etc.) but our understanding of these past events occurs in our minds in the present.

You may be wondering why I've hit you with "woo-woo" stuff at the beginning of this booklet but stick with me. Even a slight understanding of this will lead to greater freedom of thought.

It's a difficult concept to explain because we live in a world of linear time and facts – scientific "facts", historical "facts", etc. A scientist can examine a rock and tell us how old it is and where it came from. But the scientist is gathering evidence and pronouncing findings at a present moment. So everything happens in the "Now".

Your memories of the past are wholly unreliable. Your predictions of the future are usually incorrect.

There is nothing real about anything, therefore, only present experience. Your present experience of reading these words right now is all you have. Whilst concentrating on the present moment, you don't have anything else.

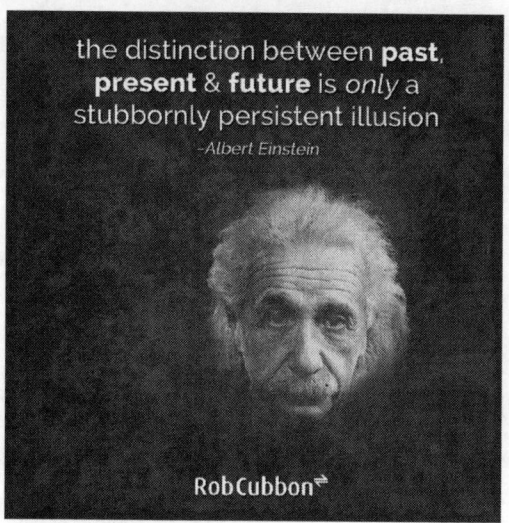

If you're not with me on this point about the past and future not existing, then don't worry. But at least let's agree that to be a happier person we need to live in the "now" more than feeling sad about the past or worrying about the future.

If you don't believe I'm a complete lunatic then discard all your previously held convictions about reality, space and time and continue on this wild journey into the present moment.

Don't Believe The Myth

Who are you? This is the myth of what most people think we are: we are human beings that popped out of a female human a few years ago, we walk the planet for a few decades and then we die.

That's all we think we are and we never question it. We think we're separate human beings even though we don't remember popping out of female humans but we assume this happened to us.

We assume there is a dividing line between us and the outside world. The outside world is there when we go to bed and greets us when we wake up in the morning. A constant presence.

What about our dreams? Life apparently includes random outside stimuli and so do our dreams. What's the difference? As far as present experience is concerned, they are exactly the same.

We experience dreaming in exactly the same way. However, we don't consider it "reality" because it's apparently crazy and doesn't make sense, even though sometimes "reality" itself is apparently crazy and doesn't make sense either. We interact with an outside world when we dream. It's exactly the same as our waking experience. Why do we believe one to be real and the other not?

What I'd like you to think about is this: you are your present moment experience.

So, as you are reading this book you are the experience of a human being reading a book. As you are talking to someone else, you are the experience of two human beings talking. And, as you are looking up at the stars at night, you are the experience of the Milky Way and other galaxies.

You are all there is because you are conscious experience.

If you haven't grasped this and you think it's too "out there" then don't worry. But I beg you to keep on reading as there's helpful stuff coming soon.

If you can at least entertain that our experience of life could be illusory and something else even more amazing is going on, then this will help you free your thoughts.

Start to see yourself as whole experiences in the present moment. For example, if you're with a group of people, see yourself as the group of people rather than as a separate person.

Try it. The exuberance of experiencing the present moment as fully as possible will contribute to your happiness more than any other one thing.

Ignore Everything You Have No Control Over

I used to see myself as a boat adrift on the ocean – without control and vulnerable to the wind and the waves.

Something bad would happen to me and I would blame bad luck, other people or something else external to me. Now, I try not to blame anything, anyone or myself. I've stopped seeing myself as separate from the world.

Whether it's true or not, I now believe **I can change my thoughts, my character and my environment from the inside out.**

I now believe that if a bad thing happens, it happens for a reason. In some way, on some level, I deserved or wanted the bad thing to happen in order to teach me a valuable lesson. As I'm living as an "experience" rather than as a separate human, I have to embrace bad things as somehow necessary to my existence.

OK, I know you're thinking about car accidents, getting cancer or being the victim of some bad fortune, like an act of terrorism for example. What did people do to deserve bad fortune or how should they embrace that? Let me explain.

A lot of the suffering I'd been experiencing was as a result of comparing myself to other people and worrying about what other people thought of me. I would always look at other guys and conclude that they were more successful, happier, better-looking, etc., and I would hate them because I thought they thought that they were better than me. It was an example of negativity that could quickly spiral out of control.

So instead of thinking about or comparing myself to others, I concentrated on myself. I compared myself to the "me" from a few months or years ago, and as soon as I found myself thinking about other people I would stop and reframe the thought.

There is no way you can know what other people are thinking or feeling. They could seem happy, successful or good-looking but you have no idea what they're feeling inside.

I kept realizing this: thinking about what other people are thinking is a waste of time. You can't completely understand other people, you can only empathize and feel compassion.

So I continued to watch my mind and tried to eliminate all unnecessary thoughts. Your brain is a marvellous tool, but 99% of your thinking – the mental static that accompanies you throughout your life – is completely pointless.

Not only is it pointless, it also causes suffering.

All suffering comes from our brain's inability to accept the present moment.

"So we should just accept terrorism and cancer? That's ridiculous!" I understand my opinions run counter to what our culture tells us. But I'm looking at it on a personal level.

If I had the ability to stop someone from committing an act of violence against others, I'd like to think I would do that. However, I see no point in worrying or even discussing terrorism as it adds to the mental anguish associated with it.

Similarly, if I was able to help a sick person or cure diseases, then I would. In fact, I do try to help people through my work. But I don't spend any time ruminating about violence, accidents or diseases because that causes suffering and doesn't help anybody.

Often our thoughts cause depression or anger and then create bad situations. Everything starts with a thought, as we've said. Monitoring thoughts and stopping the negative ones is extremely enlightening. Watch your thoughts and you will see.

Before, I would replay over and over unpleasant experiences that I'd had. Sometimes I would imagine alternative outcomes.

Even though I was trying to make myself feel better by thinking about the good things that *could have* happened, it occurred to me that this was irrelevant and possibly damaging as well. So I tried to cut out this sort of "fantasy thinking".

I don't want to confuse "fantasy thinking" with affirmations and visualisation which I'll come to later.

If you are having recurring negative thoughts and limiting beliefs then I would advise you to contact Neuro-Linguistic Programming (NLP) or Emotional Freedom Technique (EFT) specialists or groups in your area because there are some great and quick methods to get rid of them quickly.

For now, we can reframe these negative thoughts or, even better, just instantly kill them by concentrating on the present.

And, remember, don't blame yourself or anyone or anything else when negative thoughts arise. Just go back to the present moment.

Breathe.

If you see yourself as indistinct from the outside world, you are a part of other people and they are a part of you. You are more likely to want to help them and less likely to want to hurt them.

Otherwise, if you hurt someone or cause negativity in someone's life, you are adding pain or negativity to your own life. If you believe you are the experience you are experiencing at the moment, it is natural to keep that experience good or improve it. You are the experience – not the experiencer.

As soon as I decided that my business's primary aim should be to help people, rather than to make money, things got easier for me.

Concentrate on elevating your thoughts to improve your life and you will naturally improve the lives of people around you.

But, and it's a big BUT, there are loads of trapdoors here. Make sure you love people unconditionally. Try to treat people well, but don't react if they don't respond to your best behavior in the way you'd like. It's so easy to let negativity in through a trapdoor when you are trying to become more positive.

"*I smiled at him and he just looked blankly at me! Unfriendly git!*"

"*She doesn't care about other people the same way I do – she's selfish!*"

Care about your own present moment experience and ignore everything else.

"All that we are is the result of what we have thought. The mind is everything. What we think, we become." ~The Buddha

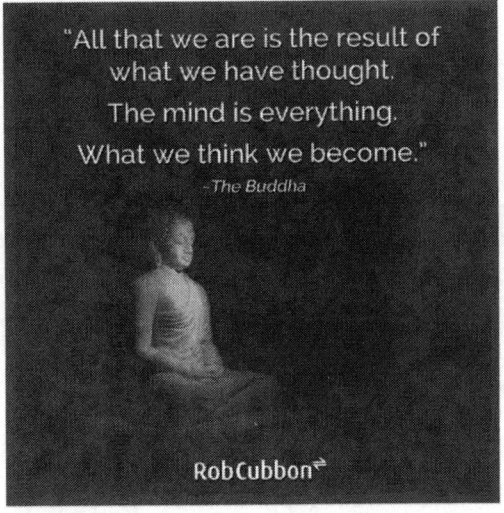

Moonbeach Bungalows, Phangan Cove, Koh Phangan

A few days after Bangkok, I'm settled in a secluded bungalow overlooking a beautiful cove in Koh Phangan – the sister island of Koh Samui in the Gulf of Thailand.

The accommodation is everything I want it to be. It's secluded enough for me to work outside but I can sometimes see the odd person walk past on the beach below me. The Wi-Fi is OK, the bathroom is clean and it has a desk and chair for working on the balcony.

I sit on the balcony with a bottle of water and start writing on my laptop.

I'm not the only one to be so fortunate. There are plenty of others like me wandering the world's most beautiful places while maintaining digital businesses. And, as you might imagine, we use the Internet to communicate. So wherever I am, I know the best places to stay, to eat at, to work quietly in, where to party, or where to relax. If I've got nothing to do, I can even find a bunch of them to hang with.

These "digital nomads" are a mixed bunch. They include everyone from the most advanced entrepreneurs building cutting edge businesses to the most inexperienced teenagers with only their laptop, a few thousand dollars and not much of a clue what to do next.

But that shows you the problem with labels. We are pigeonholed from a very early age: "little Robbie is good at English but not good at Math."

We then become "accountants," "dentists" or "thieves" – as if those individuals are interested in accounts, teeth or stealing – and nothing else. To add a label to a label: labels are ridiculous (although, sadly, necessary for communication).

Now that I've successfully unshackled myself from my "employee" label, I make money selling the products I want to make. I don't want to step into another label – even one as broad as "digital nomad" or whatever. Call me what you will, but the whole point of my current existence is to do what I want to do, where and when I want to do it.

An ability to think outside the labels definitely helps if you want more freedom and happiness in your life.

A Life Outside Labels

One of the first books I had to read in University was by the linguist Ferdinand de Saussure.

It contained some concepts which I found hard to get my head around. This 19th century Swiss guy was saying that language was a barrier between us and the world. Monsieur de Saussure was saying that the world wasn't made up of distinct isolated objects that language presupposes it is.

Confused? I was.

For example, many languages do not differentiate between certain colors on the spectrum and do not have separate terms for blue and green.

The boundaries between blue and green are not the same in Welsh and English. The Welsh word *glas* is usually translated as "blue" but it can also refer to the color of the sea, grass or even silver.

Arabic has separate terms for blue and green, however the color of the sky is sometimes referred to as "green" in Classical Arabic poetry.

We have arguments for when blue merges to green. In English there is the word "turquoise" and people rarely agree on what that is.

There is a range of light wave frequencies that most humans can see. The "colors" within the visible spectrum, what we consider to be red, yellow, blue, etc., are arbitrary (or "man made") labels that we use to attempt to explain reality.

But words always fall short when explaining reality. Just as I may say "green" to a Welsh guy and he thinks I mean "blue," words will always be pigeonholing a reality that cannot be pigeonholed.

No two greens will ever be the exact same. The color of a single blade of grass will be different from the tip to the stem. It will be lighter or darker depending on the amount of sunlight shining on it. And to add to the mystery, how do we know if the green I see is the same as the green you see?

To accurately describe the outside world we may need trillions upon trillions of words for every shade and hue of color within the visible electromagnetic spectrum.

And that's just colors. All words are similarly subjective and cannot be trusted to explain the world. When does a flower become a shrub and a shrub become a tree? One person's shack would be another person's shed would be another person's hovel and another person's home.

When does happiness turn into joy? When does anger become fury? What's the difference between sadness and depression? Why are some girls pretty and others beautiful?

It's "in the eye of the beholder," right? But us beholders are difficult to pin down as well. We change our minds frequently, and no two individuals look at the world from the same perspective. You may think that two individuals can agree that a tree they are both looking at is a big tree, for example, but that's relative to the size of the other trees that they've seen. It's a relative label and not objective.

There is no objective reality that we can be sure about.

There are no answers.

Language is a useful and, in fact, essential tool for interacting with human society, but language is sadly useless when it comes to accurately explaining reality.

Why does this matter? Look at your thoughts. Most of your thoughts will be formed by words. You walk the planet putting labels on everything: "oh look, that bridge is really big!" We see the world through the prism of our thoughts, through the filter of unreliable language.

The way that we experience reality alters our perception and reaction to it. If we can't even be sure of our version of reality, how on earth can we interact with it in a sensible way?

Try to walk around observing the world and try not to add labels. Concentrate on your experience not your thoughts. This will add to your freedom and happiness.

How Does This Help Us?

Understanding that life as largely an illusion has helped me in many ways.

It helps to see how language, generalization and prejudice cause so many difficulties.

Language forms our thoughts to such an extent that it actually distorts our versions of reality. Many arguments about all sorts of topics usually descend into arguments about definitions of words. The fact that words mean different things to different people shouldn't surprise us – we all see the world differently. And yet we all believe that everyone should see the world exactly the same way we do.

Discovering this simple fact – that everyone has a map of the world and everyone's map is essentially unreliable – is a source of freedom of thought and gives me a wonderful feeling of liberty.

Realizing that thought and language are highly subjective and unreliable ties in with positive thinking. If I experience a bad thought, I can discount the negativity instantly as unreliable and unreal.

You may ask if all thoughts are unreliable, then isn't positive thinking unreliable as well? Well, yes. Positive day-dreaming or "fantasy thinking" isn't that useful either. But positive affirmations are useful, and far more real.

Ignoring all arbitrary and subjective thought introduces great freedom in your life. I've discovered that the majority of my thoughts are completely redundant and useless.

The next chapter contains examples of the actions, unnecessary thoughts and wasteful emotions that I have tried to cut from my life. This results in more time and energy for the things I like to do.

Do the Following to Free Up Time and Energy

Don't watch the news. Bad things happen. Hearing that another bad thing just happened is a stressful waste of your time and energy. If you can stop bad things from happening, then stop them. Otherwise, constant confirmation of the existence of bad things will not help you or the people they happen to.

Don't watch TV. So, the news is out. But so are game shows, soaps, reality TV, comedies, dramas, kids' TV, etc. It's all a complete waste of time.

Don't buy or read newspapers. Newspapers, like TV news, are another delivery mechanism for more biased opinions about bad things happening in the world. They serve other people's agendas; not your own. Avoid the websites of newspapers and media companies for the same reason.

Now that you have no opinions about the news, the bad things, or the latest reality TV shows, etc., you'll have nothing to say to anyone. You may think that'll make you a boring person no one will want to talk to. But, don't worry, you'll find that a new type of person will find your positivity attractive.

Which brings me to my next point...

Lose your friends. Do you have "friends" that use you as a sounding board for their latest problems? Do you feel exhausted after talking to them? I know this advice is difficult to follow. But, *get rid of negative people from your life!*

This may be difficult, or even impossible, if negative people are in your immediate vicinity (like your family). But I have moved on from negative people in my past and it's taken a huge weight off my shoulders.

Don't blame anyone or anything. Bad things will happen to you. Use the bad things as opportunities to exercise your problem-solving muscles.

Don't worry or anticipate more bad things happening. Shit happens. Look forward to the bad things and bad people that may come into your life. They will challenge you and you will learn from them.

Don't judge people. Judgment is the source of all your problems and wasted energy.

There's no such thing as a bad person or a bad thing. The things we judge as "bad" stem from our perception of the present moment.

"Good" and "bad" are human inventions. Try to imagine anything bad happening in the universe before human beings. After humans invented language we have the first wars and violence. "Good" and "bad" were inventions of language. Before language there was no "good" or "bad", things just happened.

The story in the Bible of Adam and Eve eating of the Tree or Knowledge of Good and Evil and their subsequent fall from paradise refers to the invention of language.

You can get back to paradise and free yourself from the illusion of language by cutting down on judgment.

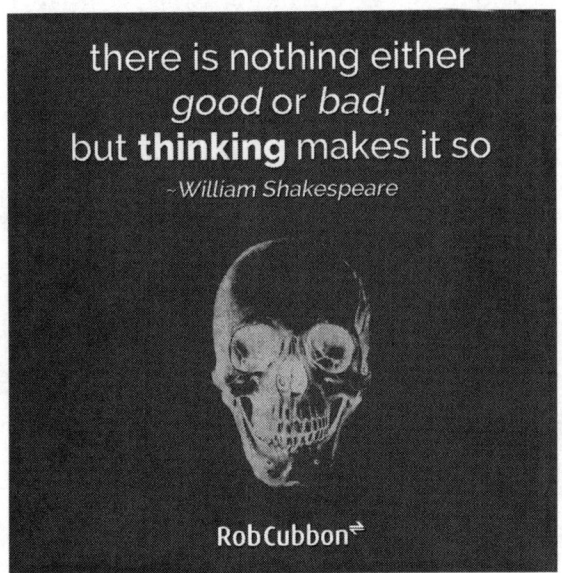

You'll never be totally free of judgment but you can try. If you find yourself judging someone, know that they're someone's mother/father, son/daughter, sister/brother or wife/husband/lover. They love and are loved.

Don't hate. Hate is a negative emotion and will cause you harm every time you feel it.

Don't complain. This is a huge time and energy win.

I used to complain a lot: when airlines lost my luggage or when solicitors over-charged. It's a waste of time. Maybe I got my money back but it was a hollow victory. It cost me more in negativity and stress.

People say, "If you don't complain, nothing will improve." Nothing has improved. People are still complaining as much now as they did when I was a kid.

Whatever you complain about will increase. What you resist persists.

Look at when a government has a "war on drugs" or a "war on terror" – drug use and terrorism only increase. Even a "war on disease", a completely laudable aim, has produced strains of super resistant bacteria that may cause new epidemics.

If you can improve peoples' lives you should, of course. Car safety and anti-smoking campaigns from the 60s and 70s undoubtedly improved and saved lives. But these came from selfless desire to do good. A rage against an abstract enemy is doomed to failure.

Complaining is all about your ego. It's revenge for a perceived mistreatment. Revenge is wasted energy and counter-productive.

Don't identify with abstract concepts. We've seen that words are arbitrary labels that describe the world very badly even when they're describing proper nouns like "tree" or "mountain". Words do an even worse job when they describe things we can't see like "communism", "terrorism", "the US", "the UK", "Buddhism", "Christianity", etc.

These things don't exist. I realize this is going to make me extremely unpopular with some people and I hate to be bearer of "bad news" but everything we build our identities on doesn't exist. (Don't worry, because "bad news" doesn't exist either!)

Countries don't exist. There's usually nothing on their borders to say what they are. They exist only in people's minds, on maps and in legal documents. But they don't actually exist.

Political movements don't exist. They "exist" as abstract ideas in peoples' minds (and most people won't agree on what they stand for) and they exist as words written on paper. But they don't actually exist.

Religions don't exist. Again, they are ideas inside various peoples' minds (again, these ideas vary wildly within religions) and they exist as words written on paper. But they don't actually exist.

They are just words – words whose meanings no two people will agree on. And yet they are responsible for most of our wars and millions upon millions of violent deaths.

Do you want a war in your life? No? So don't identify with abstract concepts, then. You may want to identify yourself as a human from planet earth if you need an identity. (But that wouldn't be correct either!)

Stop beating yourself up. We'd all love to be a good person, do good things or follow our self-imposed rules to the letter. But, you're human. You will err. You will sleep in, get annoyed, eat a burger or fail in some way. But if so, don't worry. It happens. It's OK. Really.

Don't take my advice. I realize I'm sounding prescriptive here by saying "do this" and "do that." They're just suggestions. Here's one more "do": do what you think is best.

Look at the successful and happy role models you have. Do you see them getting angry, being petty or gossiping? No, you don't. There's a reason for that.

You too can be happier and more successful by just aping the characteristics of those who are happy and successful. It's not a complete "solution" but it does make a difference.

The more I travel, the more I see how locals and foreigners are affected by news, press and government propaganda from their countries. It's frightening to know that I have opinions and judgments that I think of as my own but that have actually been given to me by years of brain-washing and exposure to the media of my country.

I know we'll never be free of cultural conditioning, but I've tried to not leap to conclusions or judge people who're different from me. Cutting down on judgments and unhooking myself from cultural, family and national conditioning certainly frees my mind and allows me to concentrate on what's more important.

Meditation

At the same time as I was trying to reduce my negative thinking, I also started a meditation practice. I still meditate every day and I'm convinced that meditation has helped me more than anything else. It's helped me physically, mentally, spiritually and psychologically.

The benefits of meditation are too numerous to list in this booklet but here are a few. Meditation will:

- Lower your blood pressure.
- Lower your cholesterol level.
- Make you sleep better.
- Make it possible for you to sleep less.
- Increase your productivity.
- Strengthen your defenses against disease.
- Even out your moods.
- Increase your emotional intelligence.
- Give you more time and space to deal with challenging people and situations so that you are better able to cope with life's difficulties.

In 2006, I met and married a beautiful woman, and my life suddenly changed. Before that, I was essentially on my own, but now I had another person around. Unfortunately, I stopped my daily meditation practice at that time.

She's still a beautiful person, but unfortunately our childless marriage failed in 2012 and I immediately started meditating again. I knew I was going to need it, and I have been meditating daily ever since.

When I started meditating I immediately stopped smoking 20 cigarettes a day. I woke up one morning, looked at some cigarettes on my living room table and thought, "I really don't want to put one of those in my mouth and light it." So I stopped smoking that day and I've never smoked since. There were no side effects. I had tried to give up smoking many times before and found it too difficult. However, by the end of that day, when I looked down at the half-finished pack on my living room table, I knew I'd smoked my last cigarette.

So, who knows what meditation will do for you?

How to meditate

Meditation is easy to start. You should only do one or two minutes of meditation at first. Any more time could be frustrating.

This is what I do. I sit down on a chair. I try to keep my back straight and let my head rest centrally upon it. Both feet are flat on the ground. My hands are in a comfortable resting position on my lap. I make sure my body is relaxed and I gently close my eyes.

I focus my awareness to the feeling of breath going through my nose.

Sounds simple enough?

Try it now!

You will notice that it's actually quite difficult to concentrate on your breathing for longer than a split second or so.

When you find that your mind has wandered, don't beat yourself up about it. This will happen *a lot*. Instead, simply realize that this has happened and put your awareness back to your breathing.

I find that counting the breaths at the start is useful. 1, 2, 3, 4, and when you get to 10, start again at 1.

As you might imagine, it's not as easy as it sounds. You will have questions about your technique. You will think you're getting it "wrong" in some way. You may get frustrated.

When that happens, bring yourself back to the present moment awareness of your breath and don't have a go at yourself.

Don't expect anything either. When you're meditating, you may feel nicely relaxed but don't expect lightning bolts of enlightenment. However, you will experience positive changes in your life after you've been practicing for a few weeks.

Maybe you'll lengthen the daily practice from a few minutes to ten minutes after a few weeks. You'll want to do it longer when the time is right for you. It's never boring.

Although you may not be the best meditator in the world, you are at least doing yourself some good. Keep trying. Keep concentrating on your breath (or whatever present moment experience you are concentrating on).

The first thing to learn is to keep at it, no matter what. It doesn't matter if you've spent five minutes thinking about soap operas, don't get angry or judge yourself, just put your concentration back to the experience of the present moment.

When do I meditate?

You should try to meditate every day at the same time of the day.

The morning is generally considered to be the best time. After you have woken up and washed but before breakfast is good because your mind is fairly clear, you have just rested and you haven't eaten yet. Meditating after you've eaten can cause drowsiness.

But any time that works is OK. You can meditate right before you go to bed. When I was living in London, I found this to be the best time.

If you are tired you will find meditation will send you to sleep. This isn't the end of the world as you will get a nice rest and realize that you now have a great cure for insomnia.

The important thing is that you set aside some part of the day for your meditation.

Where should I meditate?

By now you should be recognizing a theme developing: "try to keep things consistent, but if you don't manage consistency, don't worry!" It's the same with the location of your meditation.

I like to go to the same room in the house, sit in the same chair, in exactly the same location every time, but naturally I can't do that while I'm traveling to different places all the time.

You could also choose the room by making sure it's the quietest in the house, the room with the least light when the curtains are drawn or the room with the fewest electrical appliances. Always turn off any electrical appliances in the room and make sure your phone (on silent) isn't in the room. Try to make sure that nothing can disturb you in this room.

A personal description of meditation

Meditation is **present moment non-judgmental observation or awareness.** That definition may not seem like much, but it's incredibly powerful.

The present is where we live. In fact, we have always lived in the present and we always will. You are reading these words of this book now, in the present. This morning, when you got out of bed, you were living in the present moment. These concepts have been discussed for centuries by philosophers, sages and meditators.

Sometimes, you may think you live in the past as you find yourself endlessly reliving past events in your thoughts. You also may find yourself endlessly ruminating over future fantasies and fears – like *what if _____ happened?*

Regardless of whether our minds are thinking about the past or the future, we are always in the present – and meditation is concentration on the present moment.

Meditative experience differs from ordinary present moment experience because meditative experience is non-judgmental.

We're always labeling and judging our experience. If you take your eyes away from this book and look at your surroundings now, you will probably see a room, a few chairs, a window, sky, walls, and objects. Your eyes saw the surroundings but your brain immediately identified the objects within the experience. This happens constantly and within fractions of a second. The labeling of objects happens so immediately that we often confuse our judgements with reality. We get so confused we think the map is the territory.

Our judgments are the reason for all our suffering.

Discussion of meditation is inherently difficult because it attempts to explain with words what can only be experienced without words or concepts. Words are, in fact, little more than judgments.

Confused? It doesn't matter.

There is only conscious experience. There is only now. All we're experiencing now is all there is. There is no past; no future. Just this.

Meditation helps us accept the present moment and fall in love into it. By concentrating on the experience of the present moment we become one with it.

This is some more "woo-woo" stuff so let's lighten the mood.

None of this is important when it comes to meditation. In fact, nothing is really important at all. Just this present moment. That's all you've got. And, as long as you're concentrating on it, you're meditating.

That's it.

And remember, don't beat yourself up over it just because your mind strays. It will.

Also, don't expect anything extra special to happen to you just because you're meditating. It will. Just not in a way you'd expect.

Affirmations

We're darting back-and-forth between meditation, watching your thoughts, positive thinking, ignoring generalizations, etc., and now I'm going to throw another "airy fairy" subject into the mix. And you may be thinking, 'how is this going to help me get more freedom and happiness in my life?'

I was skeptical too, but I guarantee you'll find some positive benefits by introducing these practices into your life. (And please try to introduce one or all of these practices into your life as a result of reading this book, it'll be a waste not to!)

As I said in the beginning, everything starts with an idea. It's easier to get what you want when you know what you want – when you have a clear set of goals.

What you want

Here are some examples of goals that aren't clear:
- "I want to be happier"
- "I want more money"
- "I want motivation to do something!"

I used to have dreams like these. They are all understandable, but they are classic examples of wishful thinking from someone who doesn't know what they want.

We might think we know what we want but often we don't.

How do we find out what we want? The answer is in the previous section on meditation. Meditation gets you in a very relaxed state where you're more connected with your subconscious and who you really are. When you are in this relaxed state, it is a good time to ask yourself what you really want.

Keep your eyes closed after meditation. After your mind has been focused on your breathing for a while and you are nicely relaxed, calmly ask yourself what you want for your life.

Try it now! You'll be surprised because it will be completely different to the "money now!" thoughts you have when you're stressed or upset.

When I did this, I discovered I wanted to help people rather than make a lot of money. Suddenly I felt more attuned to my life. Now, I have purpose and motivation because I know deep down what I really want.

Another important fact about my new goals (that were centered on helping people) was that they weren't totally selfish. Farnoosh Brock, author of The 8 Pillars of Motivation, explains that if your purpose in life is more centered around helping people, you're more likely to be successful and congruent while carrying out your work.

If you are focused on helping people, you'll be more able to realize your dreams than you would if they're all about yourself.

This ties in with not seeing yourself as a separate human being. You are a family, a community, a world, a universe.

This shift helped me find my purpose in life, a direction for my business and a clear set of objectives.

Yes, I wanted enough money to survive, to live comfortably and to keep up with monthly payments. But to be honest, I'd always earned enough money. I didn't need much more.

I remember one day hearing about Paul McCartney just after he'd experienced sudden success with the Beatles in the early sixties. Since he was from an extremely poor background by today's standards, an old friend asked him what it meant to suddenly have more money.

Apparently Paul said that it didn't make any difference. He said, "I can only wear one shirt at a time, I can only eat one meal for dinner."

It's a great way of looking at money. What are you going to do with more money? Are you going to start wearing five shirts at once? Do you want to eat 10 times this evening?

Maybe you're convinced that more money will solve all your problems. Ask yourself what more money actually means to you. You might find that what you really want is freedom and happiness.

Usually, everyone who says that they want more money actually wants the freedom to do what they want, where they want, when they want. Money doesn't come into the picture.

I've managed to be free to do what I want, where I want, when I want, and it all started with this mindset shift. After this mindset book about freedom of thought, I'll write other books about financial freedom. But don't skip this stage.

How to set an affirmation

So, how do we make affirmations that can help us realize our dreams? Some people advocate writing them down, putting them in an envelope and keeping them in a special drawer. I think that is a great idea, however, I have had more success with another method.

The way I do affirmations is exactly the same as I said a few paragraphs back: wait until you're in a very relaxed state at the end of a meditation session. You're feeling relaxed, happy in your own skin and at one with the world. This is the time you should repeat your affirmation mentally to yourself. You can say it aloud also, if you want.

Make sure you're feeling good. Make sure you're feeling good about the affirmation. In fact, you should actually feel as if the affirmation is *true* in the present moment.

Since your meditation sessions should be daily, these affirmations should be daily as well. Daily affirmations made in a relaxed, meditative state will more easily enter your subconscious and manifest in reality.

How do we word the affirmation?

Affirmations should be super-specific and made in the present tense. You should feel inside as though they are true at the time that you affirm them.

Let me walk you through two of the affirmations I make myself each day after my meditation session. This is the first one:

I am enjoying increasing the passive profits to my business.

First of all, note that the above affirmation is in the present tense – "I *am* enjoying …" not "I *will* enjoy …"

Secondly, notice I'm saying "I am *enjoying* increasing the

passive profits to my business," not "I am increasing the passive profits to my business." I put that word *"enjoying"* in there because I don't want to over-work. Workaholism is danger for all entrepreneurs. I was concerned that if I just affirmed my profits going up, there was a chance they would go up as a result of working too hard and therefore being unhappy. I didn't want to be unhappy so I made sure that I "enjoy" the increase in profits and therefore I'll be happy about it.

Remember this is powerful stuff so you'll have to think through the ramifications of the affirmation. Make sure it's want you actually want.

And, lastly, I need to define what "passive profits" are. "Passive profits" are income your business can earn while you are sleeping.

For instance, imagine you had a property business that owned penthouses in various upmarket areas of your nearest city. That would be fairly cool, wouldn't it? Once you'd set up the tenancy agreements and sorted out the logistics, you'd collect the rents and earn money in your sleep.

This concept transfers to an online business like mine. I used to do graphic and web design for clients – this was money I couldn't earn in my sleep because I would only get paid each time I designed a website or a logo. I was swapping hours for dollars.

However, I slowly built business assets similar to the penthouses from my example. Only these assets weren't giant buildings; they were digital products like e-books and video courses. I spent a bit of time making them, but after that, they would sell every month creating a passive income stream without my direct involvement.

A few years ago, my passive profits were minimal, maybe $1000 a year. I then started making this particular affirmation every day after meditating: ***"I am enjoying increasing the passive profits to my business."*** My passive income profits the following year grew to $7000. It was a large increase, but still nowhere near what I was making from my graphic design client work.

The following year, 2013, they doubled to just over $15,000. Then in 2014, they grew to over $50,000. And in the first three months of 2015 (at the time of writing), my business has already made a total of $25,000 in passive income profits.

My goal for 2015 is a huge $150,000 – we'll see if I make that.

(If you're interested in how I'm doing with my passive income, feel free to sign up to my newsletters here: *http://robcubbon.com/free*).

So, there's an example of an affirmation that seems to have manifested into reality. Now, I must explain, that I still had to do the work. I wrote e-books, created video courses and worked hard to build my following online with free content so that I could successfully earn that income.

However, I'm convinced that the powerful affirmation I planted into my subconscious had something to do with it.

And remember, I still have to believe it's going to happen. I could have affirmed "I am a millionaire," but I don't know what it *feels* like to be a millionaire. Instead, I did know what it felt like to increase my passive income because it was already increasing (just *very* slowly).

I think that helps as well. Pick a success that you're already experiencing and affirm that it will grow exponentially.

Here's another affirmation about my business that I started more recently:

I'm enjoying helping and inspiring people to live happier lives by gaining greater financial freedom.

There are aspects of this affirmation that you'll be familiar with from the last example. You'll notice that this affirmation is also in the present tense.

When you *pronounce the affirmations in the present tense, it helps you believe they are happening now.*

So this affirmation is pronounced as though it is happening now, and sure enough, it is happening now.

Again, I've made sure that I'm going to enjoy this affirmation coming true because I don't want to work too hard and begrudge the success I have.

But otherwise, this affirmation is quite different from the other one. This time I'm affirming that I'm inspiring and helping others, whereas the other one is all about me.

Selfish affirmations can be quite hard to actualize. It's much better to tie your success to the success of other people, as you'll feel better about it.

The crux of this affirmation is helping others. I want other people to enjoy the freedoms I have. I have gained financial independence by working for myself and freedom of time and location by earning passive income.

I write a blog post every week at *RobCubbon.com* and regularly publish free information that will help other people set up and grow their online businesses. And this is very important to me.

Sure enough, almost every day, I get an email from someone thanking me for helping or inspiring them. I'm not making this up; they actually use the same words like "help" and "inspire" in their emails. It's almost as if they know about my affirmation.

What have we learned about affirmations?

So, here are my two affirmations:

I am enjoying increasing the passive profits to my business.

And

I'm enjoying helping and inspiring people to live happier lives by gaining greater financial freedoms.

If you knew an affirmation will come true, what would you affirm?

Whatever it is, be careful what you wish for. They do come true but not always in the way we think we want. We can never be sure we know what makes us happy so it's better to wish the best for everyone, not just ourselves.

Remember the rules of affirmations:

- Affirm when you are in a super-relaxed state.
- Affirm in the present tense.

- Feel as though the affirmation is already true.
- Feel good about the affirmation.
- Affirm something super-specific.
- It's better to affirm something that will help other people not just yourself.

> **Affirmations**
>
> Affirm when your mind is in a super-relaxed state
>
> Affirm in the present tense
>
> Feel as though the affirmation is already true
>
> Feel good about the affirmation
>
> Affirm something super-specific
>
> It's better if you affirm something that will **help other people** not just yourself
>
> RobCubbon

Goal Setting, Masterminding, Visualization and Metaphors

Affirmations made in a highly relaxed and powerful state work for me. But they are not the only way to help you realize the goals you want to achieve.

I set quarterly business goals on my website (*http://robcubbon.com*) and report back on whether I've achieved those goals.

Accountability is huge. You can get an "accountabili-buddy" – a peer or colleague you meet with or call regularly to set goals for the next call where you hold each other accountable. The deadline of the call coming up is a great motivation because you don't want to let your buddy down.

Another, perhaps more powerful version of this, is masterminding. A mastermind is a peer group of three, four, five or six people who meet or call regularly. On each call one member is in the "hot seat" and their goals are discussed. Masterminds are great for learning, encouragement and, you guessed it, accountability.

And finally, the techniques of visualization and metaphors can allow you to actually visualize yourself achieving your goals.

You can put visualization and metaphors into practice in exactly the same way as affirmations. You should start by meditating or getting yourself into a super relaxed state.

Then, when you're ready, you should visualize a scene in the future that is beneficial to you. This scene could be of you performing some action at a time when you're more successful than you are now. But you should see this visualization – feel it, sense it, taste it and smell it – as though it's happening in the present moment.

So, maybe you'd like to visualize the feeling of walking from your villa in the Algarve and into a sports car of your choice. Feel as though this is happening to you now, see the people you are with and the actions you're undertaking.

A metaphor is an even more involved version of a visualization.

Here is an example of a metaphor. I think of myself in a relaxed mood, sitting at a restaurant table in a beach resort, talking to a group of happy and well-motivated people. We are working together on a project that is going to help people (like the building of a hospital or an orphanage).

I can feel the sun on my back. The sea breeze gently takes the edge off the heat. I can hear the waves crashing on the nearby beach.

I'm relaxed, happy and focused. The table in front of me has a laptop on it, along with plates of exotic food, fruit juices and coffee. Sitting around the table with me are a group of amazing people. We're enjoying a discussion about our new project that will change the world for the better. A fragrance of coconuts and lemon grass fills the salty air.

What you can do

Affirmations and visualizations are essentially the same thing. They serve to program your subconscious mind to make your goals a reality.

Be really sure about what your goals are. And then when you're in a relaxed state, feel as though the desired outcomes have already come true. Feel them, touch them, see them, taste them, smell them. Completely immerse yourself in the affirmation or the visualization.

Start now, if you haven't already. And do this regularly.

Make sure you know exactly what you want because, be warned, this does work and you *will* get what you wish for.

Mind and Body

I can't write a whole booklet about the freedom of your thoughts, meditation, affirmation and happiness without mentioning the body.

The health of your body is just as important as the health of your mind.

Just as you don't want to put negative thoughts into your mind, you don't want to put crap into your body.

Just as you like to keep your mind active and healthy with meditation, reading and solving problems, you like to exercise your body.

A healthy body will help create a healthy mind and vice versa.

Do you have a daily exercise routine?

You can walk, run, play sports, or do whatever physical exercise you like. At the very least, do some aerobic workout for 30 minutes, four times a week.

Yoga and Tai Chi are particularly good as they exercise the body and the mind at the same time.

Ban Tai Bungalows, Mae Nam, Koh Samui, the Gulf of Thailand

I've just secured a whole bungalow with kitchen, spare room, living room, front porch and garden —all for 600 Thai Baht a night (approximately $18) in a secluded beach area of the island. I'm feeling pretty pleased with myself.

I'm having a shower before my afternoon beach stroll when I think I hear a noise from outside. I ignore it. Later, I hear the noise again. I quickly dry myself off, put on shorts and a t-shirt and make my way to the front porch. Someone is there.

"Can you move your motorbike from outside my bungalow, please?" says the man who's been knocking on the front door.

Maybe he's a little aggressive but I'm smugly amused that someone could care about something so trivial in such a relaxed and beautiful community. My face cracks a smile as I get ready to move my bike.

"Is something funny?" he asks. I notice him now. His face is very red and he's very angry. I recognize his accent as well – from the same provincial area of the southeast of England that I'm from.

I'd completely forgotten about the violence and depression that I'd left behind as I struggle to find words to deal with the situation. "No, sorry, mate, I just thought …"

"Well, if you don't move that bike, there'll be trouble!" Now he's very red and shaking. I think of saying something but I realize my mouth is dry as adrenaline courses through my veins. If I speak now my voice will waver and I'll show fear.

I move my bike.

Fear is an emotion that used to rule my life. I'd been in – and lost – many physical altercations in England when I was young. I did what everyone else did.

However, later I forged my own way, left negativity behind and enjoyed my life of freedom amongst positive people. I'd conquered fear, along with cowardice and depression.

At least, that's what I'd thought.

In the days and weeks that followed, the fear returned. Big time.

"I can't control my life," I thought, "I'm still at the mercy of random events. I can surround myself with positive people and think positive thoughts but I can't control who knocks at my door." I came down very hard on myself for feeling fear at that moment and for backing down in the face of mild aggression.

I fall right back in depression. I try moving bungalows, but it doesn't help. "I'm free to do what I want," I tell myself. So I try moving islands, but it doesn't help. "I'll get over it," I say to myself. Time is a great healer. So I try moving countries and jump on a plane to Cambodia, but it doesn't help.

My work suffers. The book I'm writing (this one) is left alone for days at a time.

I blame myself for my cowardice. I continually run and re-run the altercation through in my mind. I make up different outcomes. I know it's wrong. I make sure to meditate every day. It doesn't help.

I withdraw into my shell and become meeker in an attempt to avoid a similar situation happening again. I hate myself for doing this. So I become even more withdrawn.

If what you're doing isn't working, change what you're doing or how you're doing it

I don't have all the answers, but I've learned pragmatism.

I remember someone I'd interviewed for an aborted personal development podcast – Chris Delaney, a Neuro-Linguistic Programming (NLP) coach. He kindly agrees to a Skype session, and I feel better immediately.

I re-locate to Ho Chi Minh City and I'm immediately connected with Westerners and locals. All are positive, friendly and fascinating. I'm instantly put at ease in the "dangerous" Vietnamese capital.

I take the Skype call in my Saigon hotel after three very eventful, fun-filled days.

Chris re-programs me. I re-learn that everything happens for a reason and I re-remember that the painful moments in my life are there to teach me valuable lessons.

I re-realize that my life *will* contain random painful moments, and I look forward to them as challenges and chances to test my ever-growing toolbox of wisdom and life skills.

Suddenly, I'm hopeful about the future. Confidence, congruence and happiness return.

The Marriott, Cebu City, the Philippines

Finally I arrive at my destination: Cebu City, the "Queen City of the South," as it's referred to in the Philippines.

I'm here for a high-level conference / mastermind hosted by Chris Ducker – a brick-and-mortar businessman turned blogger and "virtual CEO".

I have learned that meeting successful people in your industry is one of the best things you can do in business. I try to mix and connect with positive people as much as I can. I try to improve the lives of people around me by being as positive as possible in their company. I am not just me; I am my surroundings. So it's natural to want to improve things.

However, there's one last thing I need to finish before I start the conference.

This book. I want to write a book on freedom of thought. I want other people to experience the freedoms that I've experienced so that they and their families become happier.

When my mindset improved, I was able to start my own business. I started to enjoy financial freedoms that I never imagined were possible. I stopped working for other people as my business grew. And with the passive income increasing, I was able to experience freedom of location.

So many freedoms I've gained: freedom of thought, freedom of finance, freedom of time and freedom of location.

There's one problem though: I'm finding it hard to write the book.

My constant traveling throughout Southeast Asia, the re-emergence of fear and depression, a nasty bout of sickness I picked up in Cambodia – they all added, so I told myself, to my difficulties in writing this book.

I barely managed to keep up with email while the book gathered digital dust on my hard-drive.

At the Marriott in Cebu, I kill time on Facebook before my 4pm call with Steven Aitchison, my business coach.

Steven Aitchison is a successful personal development blogger and businessman based in Motherwell, Scotland, who I've known for a few years. I first met him at special day-long mastermind session I attended in London in 2012.

I was immediately impressed with Steven. He's one of those people you instantly warm to. Steven is the embodiment of a happy family man – someone who never puts anyone down and always seeks to improve the lives of those around him.

Steven's a busy man; he runs a phenomenally successful website, multiple successful products and a Facebook page with nearly a million fans. As soon as I heard he was offering private coaching, I nearly bit his hand off to take it. It didn't matter how much he was charging for the Skype sessions; I knew the value he'd provide would make it worthwhile and I was happy to put the money in his PayPal account.

My policy of rubbing shoulders with positive people is paying off.

I'm fascinated by the advice Steven gives me on blogging and Facebook. I enjoy looking into the mind of a man whose words are read by millions.

I struggle to take notes so I can fully ingest everything he is saying. Finally we start to talk about my plans.

"The event is only a couple of days away, I'm never going to finish this Kindle book I'm writing," I moan. "I've only written 7,000 words and, at my usual rate of 500 a day, it's not going to happen!"

"OK, Rob," says Steven, "So you need to write another 5,000 words?"

I nod.

"How quick do you type? Fairly quickly, like 20 words a minute?"

I nod.

I hear Steven tapping away on his calculator. "So, that should only take you five hours. Why don't you just finish the book before the conference? Imagine how you'd feel when you've done it?"

"Yes, but, but, but… WTF??!?!?"

Steven's suggestion was as audacious as it was challenging.

I'd only ever written 500 words a day in my usual laid-back way before. I suddenly see how my laziness had allowed me to get into a terrible mental block with this book.

I finish the call with Steven and rush outside the hotel to the neighboring shopping mall, dart into the first restaurant I see (I haven't eaten anything yet). I ask the same question I've probably asked every single day the last two months: "Do you have Wi-Fi?"

"Actually, sir," replies the beautiful Filipina waitress, "it's not that good."

"Great!" I reply, and sit down to write.

Putting it all together

This was only meant to be the first few chapters in a book about freedom. It grew to a much bigger book about how a few mindset shifts helped me discover a happier life.

I started identifying negative thought patterns and stopping them dead before they could hurt me. I also found solace in semiotic, philosophical and Buddhist ideas on the nature of reality. I used meditation to improve myself physically, mentally, spiritually and psychologically and became a happier person. I experimented with affirmations and planted suggestions into my subconscious to manifest a better reality.

I am sure that you, as you've made it to the end of the book, will be able to free your thoughts and become a happier person as a result of reading this book.

If you're not practicing meditation now, please start straightaway. You only need to sit down, close your eyes and try to concentrate on your breathing for two minutes. This will be enough to add a little space inside your busy mind.

Once you've started a meditation practice (that will naturally increase as the days pass) you should start "watching" your thoughts at various times throughout the day. You will see how generalizations, cultural attitudes, judgment, worry and over-thinking can cause you suffering.

These two things alone – daily meditation and a desire to cut down on damaging thoughts – will make you happier. I promise.

Please, try it!

I urge you to not finish reading this booklet only for it to gather dust (real or digital) on your bookshelf. I beg you to take action.

The most effective action would be to attempt to control your thoughts with meditation and to stop potentially damaging thoughts by observing them and stopping them before they become limiting or harmful beliefs.

And, at the end of your daily meditation practice, you can visualize or affirm a wonderful success story that helps you and other people as well.

If any of the above has helped you, no one would be happier than me. Please let me know by the way of a review of the booklet in the Amazon store. If not, then that's totally fine. It's great that you made it to the end of the book and I wholeheartedly thank you for that.

If you have any questions please pop along to *my website* at *http://robcubbon.com* and leave a comment on one of the articles or drop me a line.

And remember, you can *sign up to my email list* to receive free newsletters, Kindles, courses and e-books. Sign up here: *http://robcubbon.com/free* – remember this is only the first book in a series. After freeing our thoughts we're going to free our finances, our time and our location. If you stay on the mailing list, you'll be informed of when you can get the other books in the series for free.

Cheers,

Rob Cubbon

P.S. Keep reading, there are more ways I can help you!

Afterward

After the conference in the Philippines I was hanging around Cebu City, tapping away on my laptop in various cafés, hotel lobbies and co-working spaces. I was working really hard, desperate to put all I'd learned into practice and trying to recruit local virtual assistants.

I still hadn't finished writing this book. The first draft had returned from the editor with loads of queries about the writing and the message I was trying to convey.

One lunchtime I got a Skype call from my brother. Lunchtime in the Philippines is 6am in the UK. I knew it was bad news.

My father had died of a heart attack that morning.

My brief sojourn around Southeast Asia was over as my life's journey took an unexpected turn. I didn't know what to think as my eyes filled with tears in the taxi on the way to the airport.

But I knew I was lucky to have my father for so long. And I knew that no man had ever done so much for me than him.

So this booklet is dedicated to Brian Cubbon, April 4 1928 – May 20 2015.

Acknowledgements and Recommended Reading

I mentioned several people and authors in the text of this book, so I thought I'd share the resources here.

First, the authors who have influenced me most in terms of being in the now, non-duality, meditation and living a compassionate life have been: Eckhart Tolle (The Power Of Now), Alan Watts (The Taboo Against Knowing Who You Are) and Byron Katie (Loving What Is). These authors are amazing. Search for them on Google, Amazon and YouTube and prepare to get your mind blown.

The book mentioned by Farnoosh Brock is *The 8 Pillars of Motivation: How to Move Away from Fear and Achieve Your Greatness.*

Chris Delaney is mentioned as an NLP and Life Coach. His website is here: *http://christopher-delaney.com/*

Steven Aitchison is a hugely successful personal development blogger and my personal business coach at the time of writing. He can be found here: *http://www.stevenaitchison.co.uk/*

Paul McCartney was a member of the 1960s popular beat combo The Beatles. ;)

The **Chris Ducker** event I referred to is here: *http://chrisducker.com/ttt-2015/*

Special thanks to the numerous people who've helped me with this book out of the kindness of their hearts. I love you all.

Not wanting to pick anyone out but special thanks to Megan Garrison, Ani Alexander, Kathryn Bryant, Jyotsna Ramachandran and Nick Loper.

This booklet is dedicated to Brian Cubbon, April 4 1928 – May 20 2015.

Many thanks to all of the above, as well as everyone who has been a part of my amazing life these past four decades.

Excerpt from one of my other books: From Freelancer to Entrepreneur: Escaping work and finding happiness

This is a semi-autobiographical book about how I was lost professionally, emotionally and spiritually and how, bit by bit, I was able to set up my own business and work from home – with a few ups and downs along the way.

You can buy this book on Amazon US: From Freelancer to Entrepreneur: Escaping work and finding happiness http://www.amazon.com/dp/B00J7BK4MC/

You can buy this book on Amazon UK: From Freelancer to Entrepreneur: Escaping work and finding happiness http://www.amazon.co.uk/dp/B00J7BK4MC/

Please find my other books here: *Rob Cubbon on Amazon.*

Chapter 1: "More by accident than by design"

I'm a very lucky man.

I was born in England to fairly well-off parents. I have both my arms and legs. I possess modest intelligence, near perfect eyesight, and I can vaguely string an English sentence together in both spoken and written form.

However, I didn't always think I was lucky. In fact, my head used to be filled with thoughts of how unlucky I was: *If only I were better looking; If only I'd been more popular at school; If only*

I'd been born with more innate talent.

This book is the story of how, in only a few years, I went from being a barely employable Mac monkey—trudging joylessly around London offices, performing mind-numbingly repetitive tasks that no one else wanted to do—to running a successful graphic design business. It doesn't center, as a lot of books do, around one transformative life-changing moment. Instead, this book contains a whole host of them.

There have been many coincidences, pieces of advice, and much wonderful happenstance. My assertion that "I am a lucky man" has actually become more true during the writing of this book.

And there are more general instances of luck.

My consciousness has attached itself to a human at this moment. That's lucky; I would hate to have been a slug, although I've always thought being an albatross would be kind of cool.

I am alive in 2014. I am alive in the Internet age, and I have the opportunity to set up an online business and to craft my own lifestyle. A few years ago, this wouldn't have been possible. I would have had to do what I was told by the boss/factory owner/feudal landlord/lord/chief/king.

And then there are more general instances of good luck. For example, my freelance work meant I had time to work at home building up my business whilst I had money coming in; it didn't matter that the business didn't bring in much in the first two years. In 2005, I was introduced to WordPress, the most popular website content management system (CMS). I started blogging in 2006. My website looked shockingly bad from 2005–2007, but it didn't matter because the recession hadn't happened yet.

I have learned to be grateful. I occasionally wake up and thank the universe for my position within and experience of it.

Chapter 2: Starting work

If you're older than eighteen, what would be the one thing you'd say to your eighteen-year-old self?

Yeah, I know; "Buy Apple stock" would be obvious. But I would actually say, "Don't bother going to college; leave that crappy band you play guitar for; don't bother getting a job. Just do what you want!"

Our schools, families, and backgrounds pre-program us, and we spend our whole lives trying to unlearn it.

That was certainly the case for me when, aged twenty-one and virtually unemployable, I limped toward the end of my higher education with a humanities degree from a lesser-known London University.

I eventually found a job, and this was—and always will be—my only job ever, as a picture researcher for a magazine aimed at the over-fifties. This was hardly the glamorous media career I'd had in mind. It was the only thing I could get in the early nineties, when the UK was going through another recession, and I was pleased with it.

The day-to-day work at that magazine would seem industrial today, and it's hard to imagine that it was only twenty years ago.

But the worst thing about my old job wasn't the mind-numbing, pointless, repetitive to-ing and fro-ing. No, it was the boss.

She seemed nice enough at first, but I'd noticed a certain trepidation in the other staff toward her. It wasn't long before I found out why. This superficially pleasant and charming fifty-something lady could morph into a mad dictator of Hitleresque proportions at the drop of a hat. She spent most of the day criticizing, haranguing, and patronizing her staff. This was a period of particularly bad recession for the middle class. Those who had jobs would hold onto them for fear of losing the homes and stability they'd spent their whole lives working towards.

The women in that office used to tell me that I was lucky to be a man because I missed the worst of her attacks.

But I'd seen enough. After a few months I was ready to get out of there. I desperately looked around for another job, but I couldn't find one. The recession had hit hard and I didn't have the skills, experience, or training that employers were looking for. Who does at twenty-one?

For two more years I was stuck in this nightmare job. It would have been difficult for me to believe this at the time, but that was probably the most educational period of my professional life. Why? The experience was so bad that it led me to become an entrepreneur.

The education came from looking at the fear on my poor colleagues' faces, frightened to do anything wrong and suffer public humiliation at the hands of the boss. I knew I could never end up like them. At one stage, I thought I'd rather be homeless and unemployed, but thankfully, I never had to find out.

You can buy this book on Amazon US: From Freelancer to Entrepreneur: Escaping work and finding happiness *http://www.amazon.com/dp/B00J7BK4MC/*

You can buy this book on Amazon UK: From Freelancer to Entrepreneur: Escaping work and finding happiness *http://www.amazon.co.uk/dp/B00J7BK4MC/*

Peace!

Made in the USA
Middletown, DE
29 January 2026

27759998R00044